What Are Angels?

Lady Kimberly Motes Doty

What Are Angels?

Lady Kimberly Motes Doty

ISBN: 9798878805223 (paperback)
ASIN: B0CPWRDGQZ (paperback)
ISBN: 9798869032836 (paperback)
ISBN: 9798869032843 (EPUB digital)
ISBN: 9798878807029 (hardcover)
ASIN: (hardcover)
ISBN: 979-8-8691-8003-2 (hardcover)

Lady Kimberly Industries, LLC

15019 Madeira Way, #86174

Madeira Beach, Florida 33708-9998

https://mybook.to/LadyKimberlyBooks

Once upon a time, there was a little boy named Cade who
loved to hear stories about angels.

He would often ask his mommy questions about
angels.

One day, his mother sat him down and shared a beautiful story that explained it all.

"Listen carefully, Cade," his mother began.

"In the Bible, there are verses that explain this to us."

Are they not all ministering
spirits, sent forth to minister for
them who shall be heirs of
salvation?
Hebrews 1:14 KJV
Lady Kimberly

"The first verse explains to us what angels are."

"It is Hebrews 1:14 and it says 'Are they not all ministering spirits, sent forth to minister for them who shall be heirs of salvation?'"

"Angels are like special beings called spirits."

"Unlike us, they don't have a physical body that we can see or touch."

"They are made up
of pure energy and
have a different
form."

"Just like how we have a body to move around and do things, angels can move and do things without needing a body."

They are kind of like invisible helpers that are always around us, even though we can't see them."

"That is so cool!" said Cade.

"The word "minister" means helping others", his
mommy continued.

"Angels are like helpers for people
who believe in God and Jesus."

"A 'ministering spirits', means angels help us believers in different ways."

"Sometimes, when we pray, God sends angels to answer our prayers."

"Angels also encourage us believers when we are feeling down or need support."

"Another important thing angels do is protect us believers."

"They keep us safe under God's watch."

"It's important to remember that only God can send angels to help us."

"Angels can't decide to come on their own."

"They are like servants to God and do what He asks them to do for us."

Cade thought for a moment,
then he asked his mommy,
"How does an Angel answer
our prayers, Mommy?"

"That's a very good question Cade!"
said his mommy.

"In the Bible, it also tells us this answer in Daniel 9:21-23. Here it tells us about an angel named Gabriel who came as an answer to a prayer for a man named Daniel."

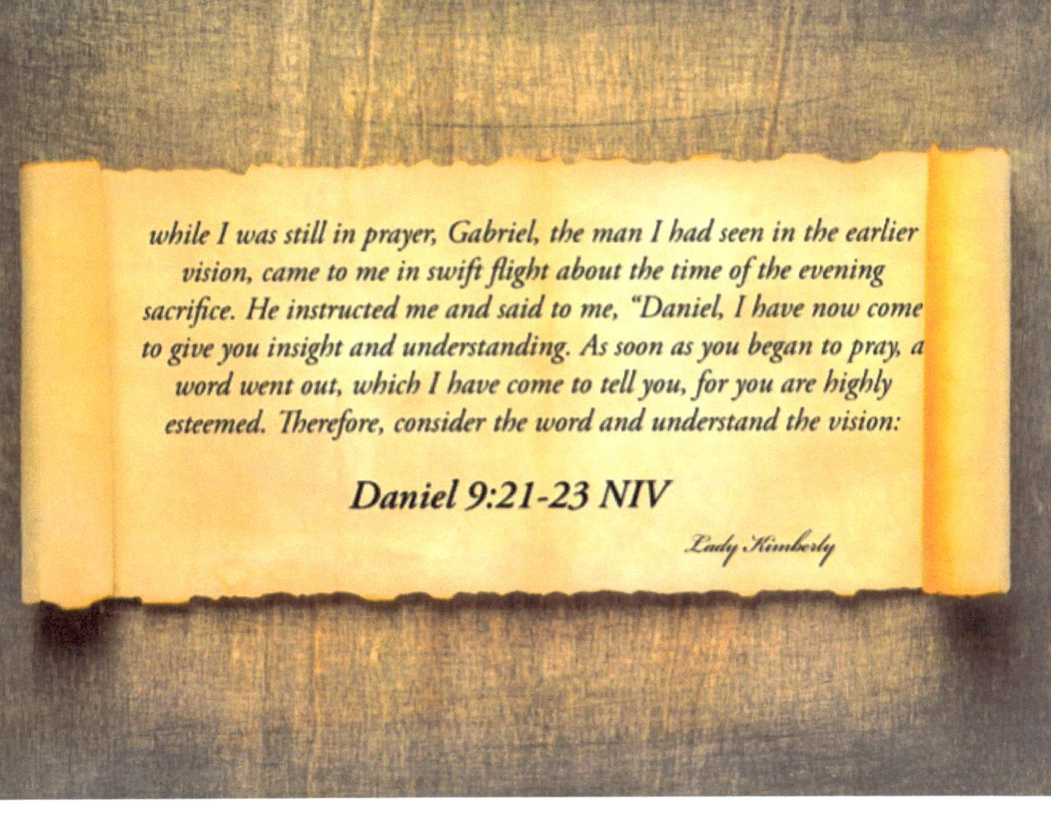

while I was still in prayer, Gabriel, the man I had seen in the earlier vision, came to me in swift flight about the time of the evening sacrifice. He instructed me and said to me, "Daniel, I have now come to give you insight and understanding. As soon as you began to pray, a word went out, which I have come to tell you, for you are highly esteemed. Therefore, consider the word and understand the vision:

Daniel 9:21-23 NIV

Lady Kimberly

"In these verses, Daniel is telling us about Gabriel, the angel's visit to him, 'while I was still in prayer, Gabriel, the man I had seen in the earlier vision, came to me in swift flight about the time of the evening sacrifice. He instructed me and said to me, "Daniel, I have now come to give you insight and understanding.As soon as you began to pray, a word went out, which I have come to tell you, for you are highly esteemed. Therefore, consider the word and understand the vision:'"

"Daniel is telling us that the angel Gabriel flew in and told him that as soon as he began to pray, his prayers were answered." Cade's mommy explained the long verses from the Bible.

Cade's imagination ran wild as he imagined the angel Gabriel flying in to personally answer his prayers!

Cade's mommy smiled and said, "I haven't heard of any angels flying in person and answering prayers anymore, Honey."

Cade still really loved the idea of an angel flying in to answer his prayers.

But he also knew his mommy was right. He hadn't heard of any angels flying around either.

If there had been any angels flying around answering prayers, it would definitely be on his online videos!

He hadn't seen anything about flying angels answering prayers online!

"Mommy, what does the Bible say angels look like?",
Cade asked.

"The Bible gives us a few different descriptions of angels, some have descriptions of angels with 6 wings",

"some angels have 2 wings",

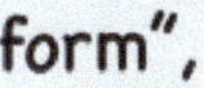

"some descriptions say the angels can take on a human form",

"and one where the angel appeared as a beam of light"
Cade's mommy explained.

"Angels can take on whatever shape God needs them
to take on! How cool is that!" Cade said excitedly.

"Tell me more about angels, Mommy", I really love
how amazing they are!", Cade encouraged his
Mommy to continue with her story about angels.

"The Bible also
tells us how
the angels
take care of
us."

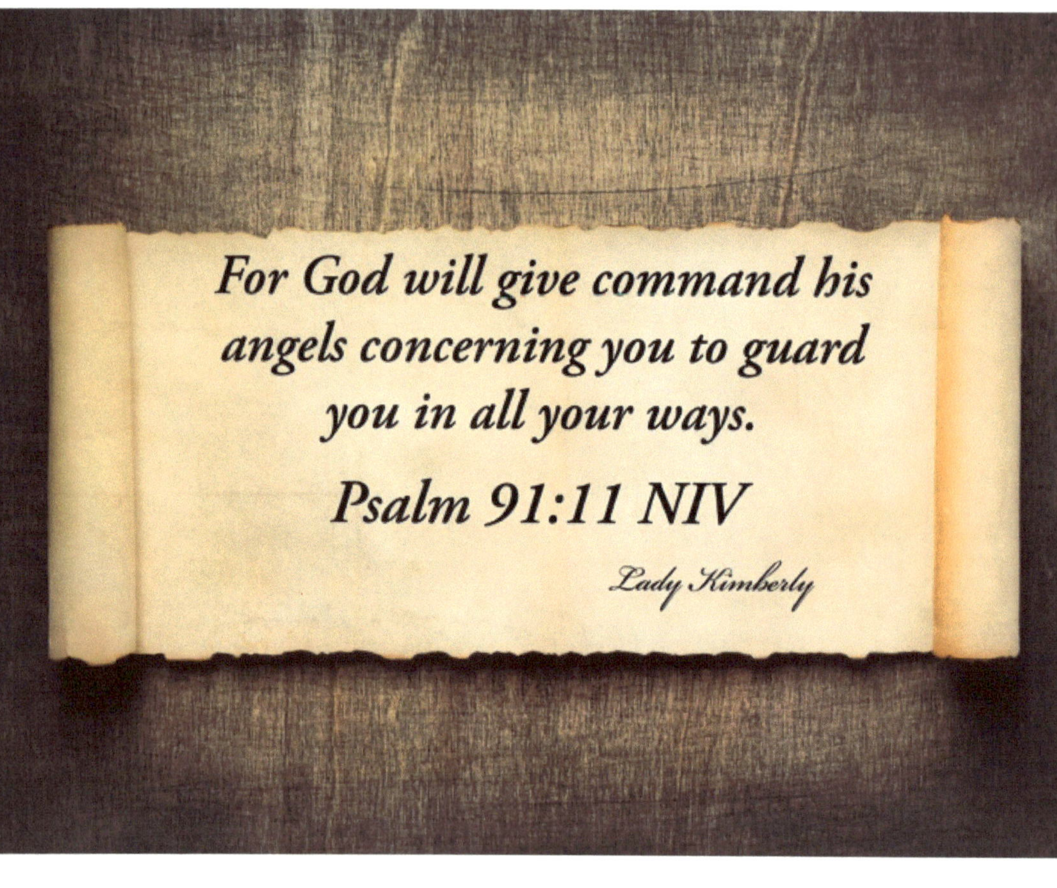

For God will give command his angels concerning you to guard you in all your ways.
Psalm 91:11 NIV
Lady Kimberly

"This means that God loves us so much that He sends angels to watch over us and protect us in everything we do."

Cade's eyes widened with curiosity as he asked, "Mommy, how do these angels protect us?"

"Can we see the angels?"

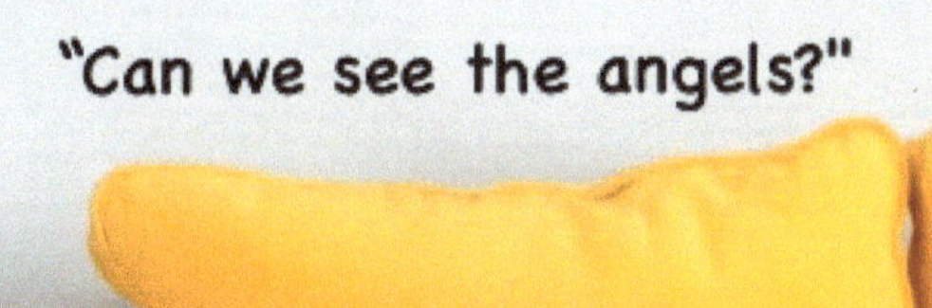

His mother smiled and replied, "Well, Cade, as we talked about, angels are special beings that we cannot see with our eyes, but we can feel their love and protection."

"They are like
invisible
superheroes

sent by God."

"When we are in danger or need help, God commands his angels to watch over us and keep us safe."

Cade looked amazed and asked, "But how do they know when to protect us, Mommy?"

Cade's Mommy continued, "In another verse from the Bible, Luke 4:10, it explains this to us where it says, 'For it is written, "He will command his angels concerning you to guard you carefully."'"

For it is written:

"'He will command his angels concerning you
to guard you carefully;

Luke 4:10 NIV

Lady Kimberly

"This means that when we trust in God and have faith in Him, He tells the angels to be with us at all times and watch over us."

"God tells them when we are scared, feeling lonely, or going through tough times, and they come to our aid."

Cade's eyes sparkled with excitement as he imagined angels surrounding him, protecting him at all times.

"Can I talk to the angels, Mommy?

Can I ask them for help?"

His mommy nodded and said, "Absolutely, Cade

God loves when we talk to Him and His angels.

You can pray
to God and ask
Him for
protection and
help.

Sometimes, you might even feel a warm presence or a sense of peace, and that is the angels letting you know that they are there with you."

Cade hugged his mommy tightly and said, "I'm happy to know that God's angels are always watching over us."

"It makes me feel safe and loved."

Cade's mommy smiled and said,
"That's the beautiful thing, Cade."

"God's love is so vast and amazing that He sends His angels to guard and protect us."

"Remember, whenever you feel scared or need help,"

"just close your eyes and ask God to send His Angels
to come and protect you and they will be right
there with you protecting you and keeping you safe."

About the Author

Lady Kimberly Motes Doty has dedicated her life to helping people in many different ways. She is a minister, which means she helps others find their spiritual path. She is also a life coach, which means she guides people to live their best lives. Lady Kimberly is even a natural health specialist, which means she knows a lot about taking care of our bodies and staying healthy. In addition to all of this, she loves to write and share her wisdom with others. When she's not working, she enjoys spending time with her family.

LadyKimberlyIndustries.com

LadyKi.com

https://mybook.to/LadyKimberlyBooks

More Lady Kimberly Children's Books for you to enjoy!

A Children's Guide to a Godly Way of Life is not just another ordinary book. It is a treasure trove of knowledge and wonder, carefully crafted to quench the thirst for understanding that resides within every child's soul. With each turn of the page, their imagination will ignite, propelling them on a lifelong voyage of love and devotion to God, and an insatiable hunger for unraveling the mysteries of the divine.

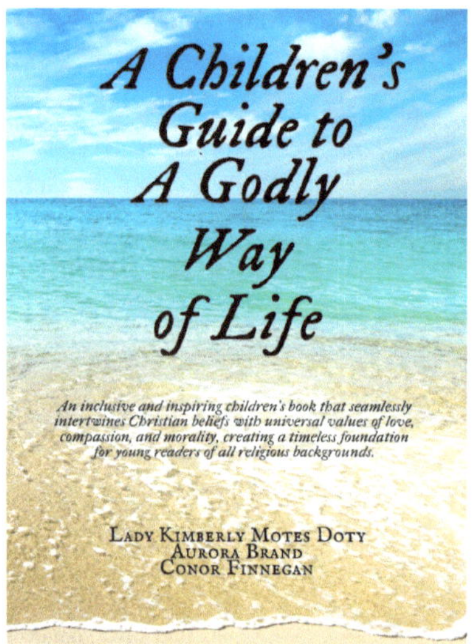

Introducing a captivating and educational new children's book series by the talented author, Lady Kimberly Motes Doty. This incredible series aims to teach children about God's love and His teachings from the Bible through meaningful and relatable short stories. Lady Kimberly Motes Doty has beautifully crafted each book to be Biblically based and easy for children to understand, ensuring that young readers can grasp the profound messages within.

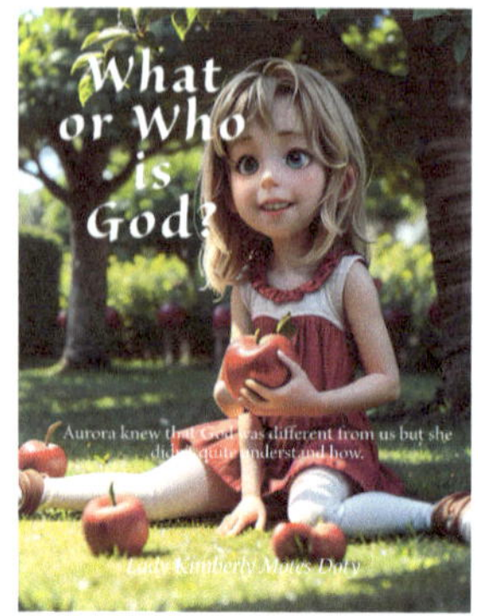

The first book in the series, "What or Who is God?", tackles the age-old question that has puzzled minds throughout history. Lady Kimberly Motes Doty introduces children to the concept of God in a gentle and relatable way, encouraging them to ask questions and explore their curiosity. Through this book, children will develop a personal connection with God, enabling them to understand His presence in their lives.

Following this, "Where is God?" takes young readers on a journey of discovery, highlighting the beauty of God's presence in everyday life. Lady Kimberly Motes Doty reminds children that although God may not be seen with physical eyes, His love and guidance are always there, waiting to be discovered in the wonders of the world and the kindness of others. This heartwarming story inspires children to explore their own connection with God, fostering a sense of awe and gratitude.

In "Does God Lie?", Lady Kimberly Motes Doty invites readers to embrace the truth that God's promises are like a treasure chest filled with love, peace, and hope. This heartwarming story reassures children that in a world filled with uncertainties, they can find solace and strength in the unwavering faithfulness of God. Through relatable characters and engaging storytelling, young readers will learn the importance of trust and the power of God's word.

Continuing the series, "Is Everything God Does Good?" explores the beauty and love found in God's creations, emphasizing the importance of being good stewards of the natural world. Lady Kimberly Motes Doty's delightful tale encourages children to appreciate and respect the wonders of the world, fostering a sense of responsibility and gratitude for God's creations.

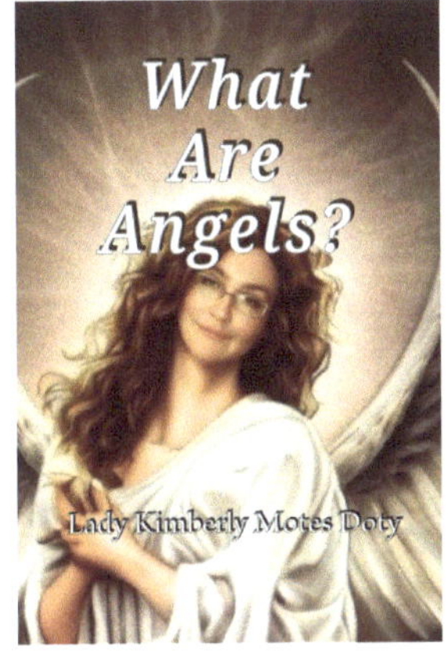

The Last book in the initial release is, "What Are Angels?" which captivates young readers with its exploration of angels and their role in our lives. Through the eyes of a curious little boy named Cade, Lady Kimberly Motes Doty takes children on a journey of discovery and understanding. Cade's fascination with angels leads him to ask his mother about their purpose and how they keep us safe. In response, his loving mother imparts wisdom and shares stories from the Bible, explaining that angels are invisible superheroes sent by God to watch over and protect us. This enchanting story instills a sense of wonder and reassurance in children, reminding them of the divine presence that surrounds them.

Lady Kimberly Motes Doty's children's book series is a true gift to young readers, offering them the opportunity to develop a deep understanding of God's love and teachings in a language they can comprehend. Each book in the series presents important lessons in an accessible and engaging manner, nurturing children's spiritual growth and fostering a lifelong connection with God. With these captivating and educational stories, Lady Kimberly Motes Doty has created a series that will undoubtedly become a cherished addition to every child's library.

The second release in Lady Kimberly's series, "Discovering God's Love" begins with "Is Anger Bad?". It is a charming tale that teaches children about the power of anger and how to handle it wisely. Through relatable characters and captivating storytelling, this book empowers young readers to embrace their emotions and make a positive impact on the world.

It continues with the uplifting children's book, "What is God's Greatest Commandment?" takes readers on another journey with the three curious and compassionate cousins Aurora, Conor, and Cade. One day, while playing near a majestic oak tree, they happen upon a special book called the Bible. As they open its pages, they discover the concept of commandments – rules given by God to guide them in living a purposeful and fulfilling life. Driven by their newfound understanding, Aurora, Conor, and Cade embark on a mission to put these commandments into action in their daily lives.

She has many more books planned for the series as the Bible contains over 600 verses of commandments with multiple commandments in each verse and an unlimited imagination to fill the pages for young readers!

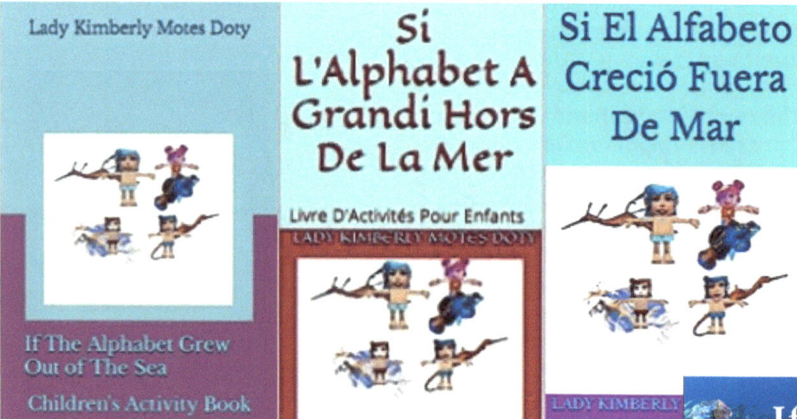

If the

Alphabet Grew Out of The Sea V1 – in English, French & Spanish

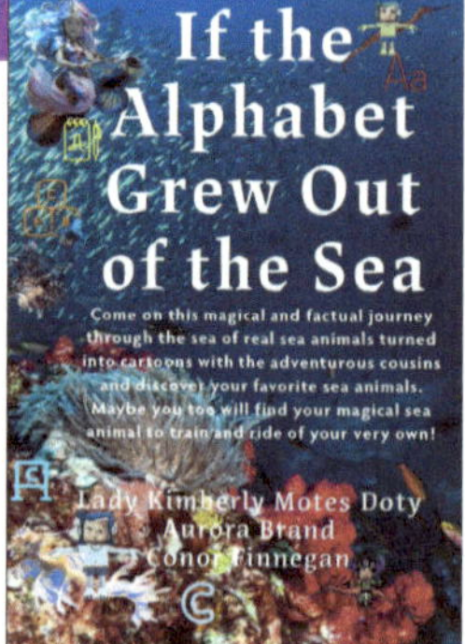

Almost 600 pages of mazes, word searches and fun sea animal facts as Aurora, Conor and Cade search for sea animals for every letter of the Alphabet!

Embark on an enchanting adventure with Conor and his wise grandmother, Mimi. Join them on a treasure hunt for the fabled Conch shell, rumored to possess a magical sound. This heartwarming tale explores the power of love and the enchantment found in simple moments. Inspired by their journey, Conor and Mimi's story inspires others to embark on their own adventures and treasure hunts. Discover the magic within the pages of "Conor's Magical Treasure Hunt.

"The Treasure Hunters: A Beachcombing Adventure"

Embark on an unforgettable beachcombing adventure with Aurora, Cade, and their beloved Mamaw. Join these adventurous siblings as they search for hidden treasures washed up by a powerful storm. From sand dollars to seashells, their journey is filled with wonder, joy, and the bonds of family. Discover the magic of exploration and the beauty of the ocean in "The Treasure Hunters: A Beachcombing Adventure."

"The Enchanted Seashell: A Magical Beach Adventure"

"The Enchanted Seashell: A Magical Beach Adventure" is a heartwarming children's book that takes young readers on an enchanting journey filled with wonder, discovery, and the power of love and resilience. Join Cade and Aurora as they embark on a treasure hunt to find the largest sand dollar ever. Along the way, they learn valuable lessons about patience, the beauty of nature, and the importance of ocean conservation. This captivating tale inspires children to appreciate the wonders of the world and make a positive impact on the planet.